Twins Activity Book

By Peg Connery-Boyd

Hawk's Nest Publishing, LLC

HawksNestPublishing.com

Major League Baseball trademarks and copyrights are used with permission of Major League Baseball Properties, Inc. Visit MLB.com

ISBN-10: 1-936562-29-4
ISBN-13: 978-1-936562-29-9

Illustrations by
Scott Waddell
www.ScottWaddellFinearts.com

Interior Layout by
Matt Haas
www.MattHaas.com

Coloring Page

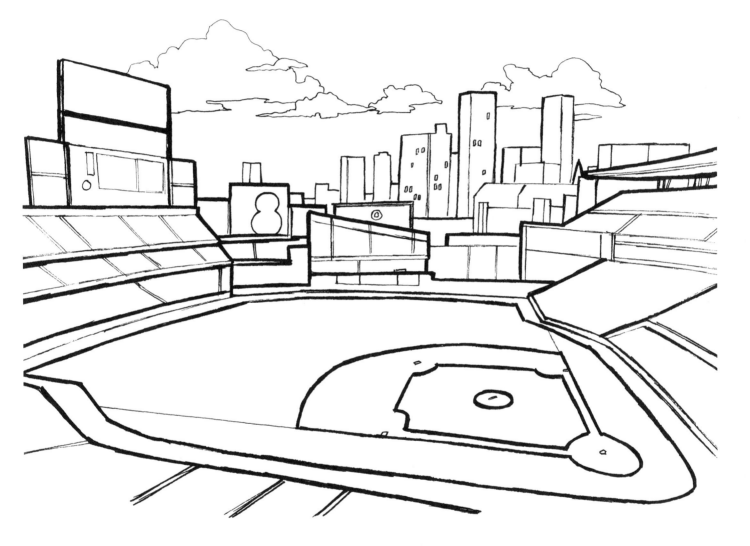

TARGET FIELD™

Retired Heroes Game

Unscramble the names of the *Twins* heroes on the jerseys below.

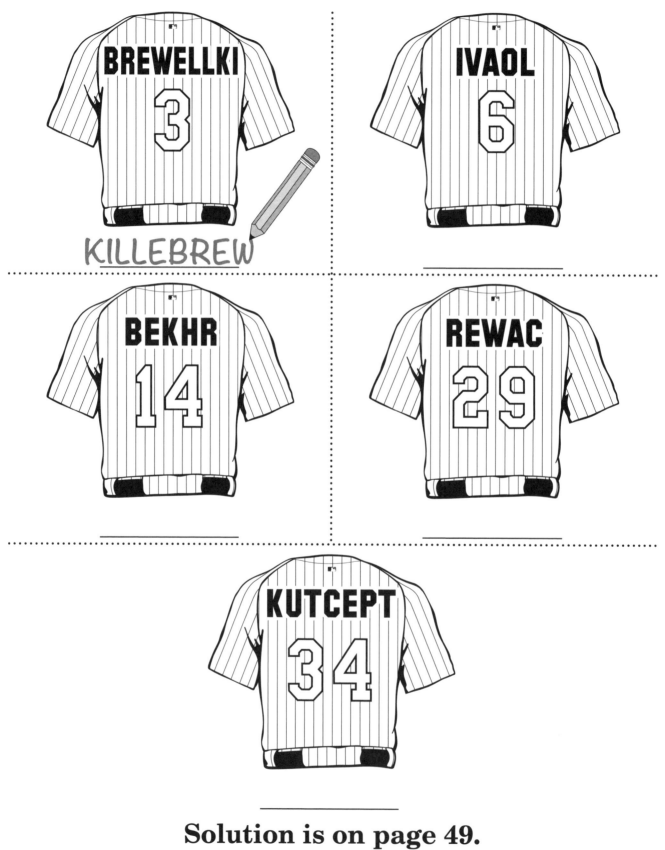

BREWELLKI
3

KILLEBREW

IVAOL
6

_____

BEKHR
14

_____

REWAC
29

_____

KUTCEPT
34

_____

Solution is on page 49.

Follow the Ball #1

Circle the pitcher that threw a strike.

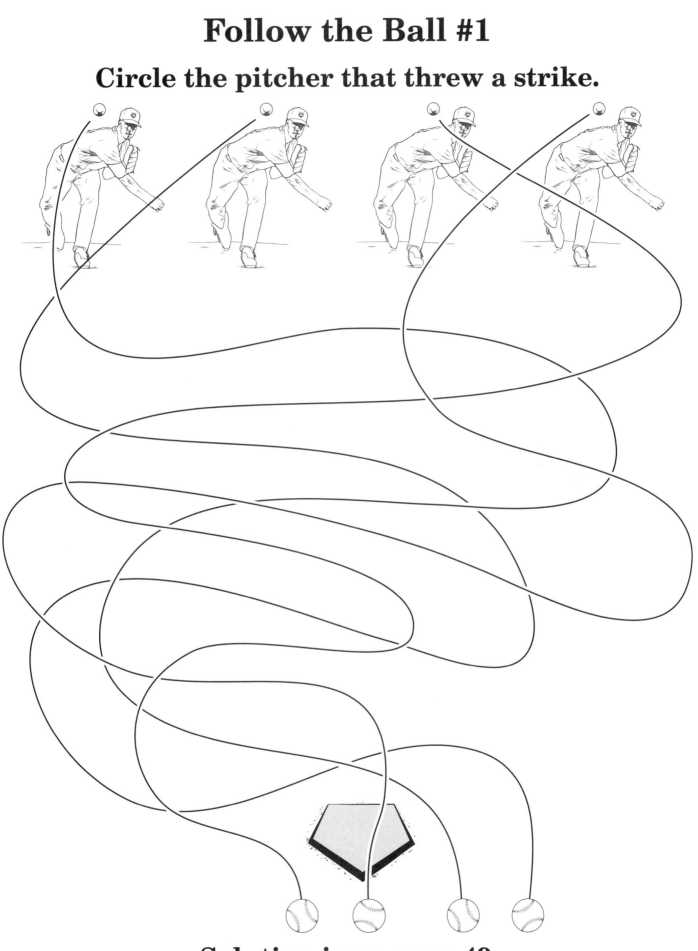

Solution is on page 49.

Connect the Dots #1

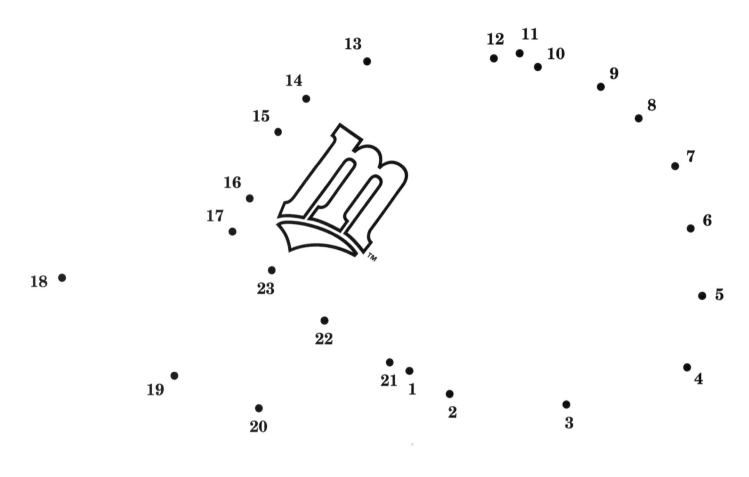

Find the Differences #1

Find three differences between the two images.

Solution is on page 50.

Maze #1

Solution is on page 50.

Find the Difference #2

Circle the image that is different.

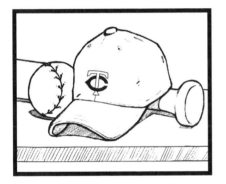  

  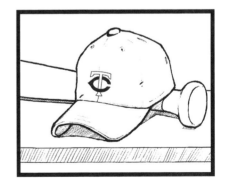

Solution is on page 51.

Draw the *Twins* Logo

Use the grid to help you draw the *Twins* logo!

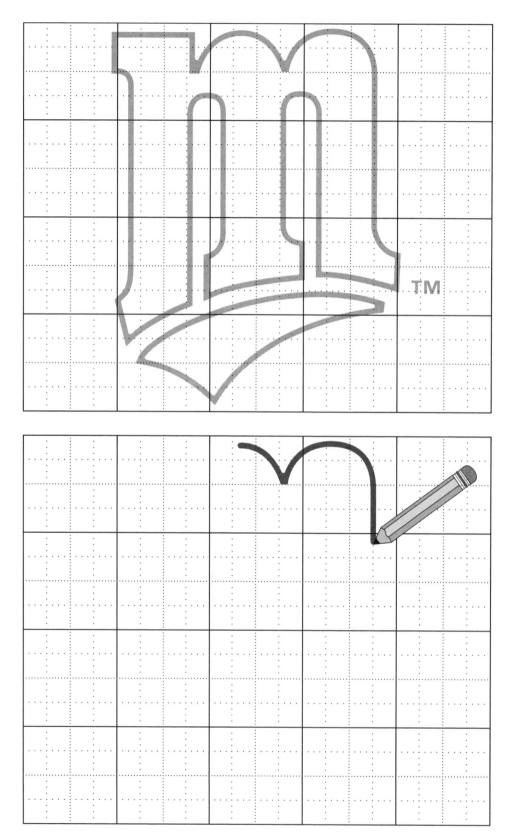

™

Secret Message #1
Use the key to unscramble this message.

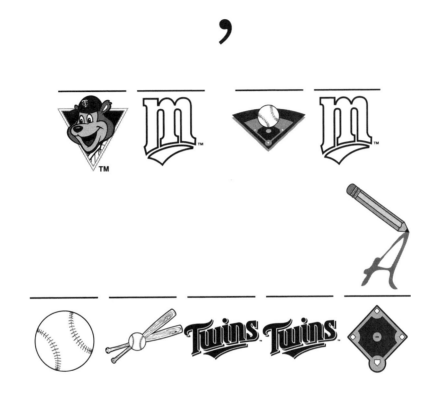

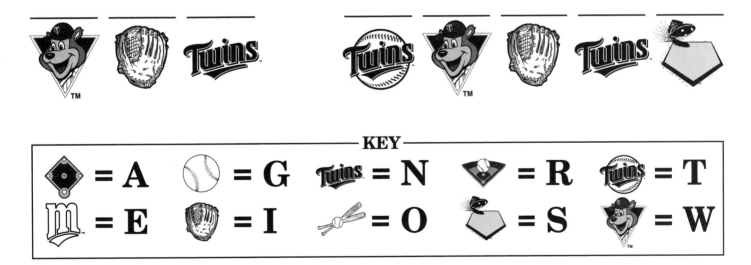

= A	= G	= N	= R	= T
= E	= I	= O	= S	= W

Solution is on page 51.

Label the Parts of a Baseball Field

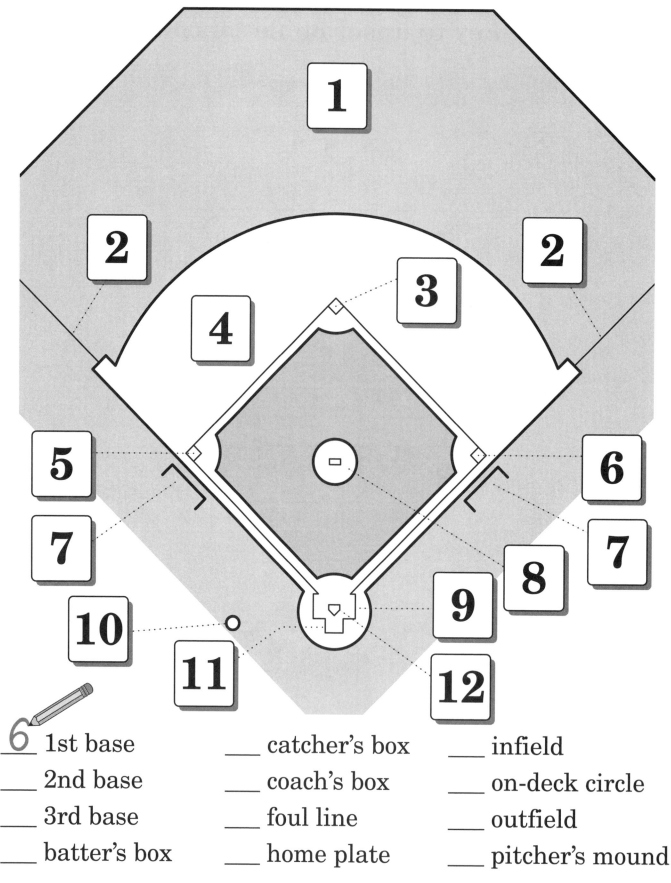

__6__ 1st base

___ 2nd base

___ 3rd base

___ batter's box

___ catcher's box

___ coach's box

___ foul line

___ home plate

___ infield

___ on-deck circle

___ outfield

___ pitcher's mound

Solution is on page 52.

Coloring Page

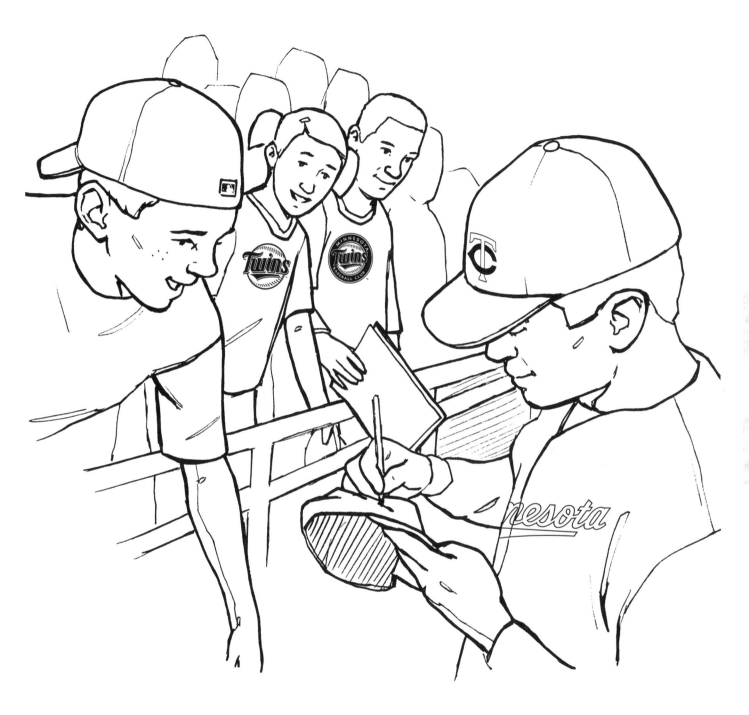

Stadium Snacks Scramble

Unscramble the letters to reveal the names of these tasty stadium snacks.

DOAS

_ _ _ _

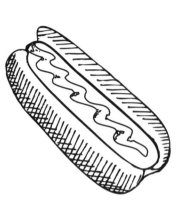

OTH GDO

_ _ _   _ _ _

ROCPOPN

_ _ _ _ _ _ _

CIE MCEAR

_ _ _   _ _ _ _ _

ZEPRTEL

_ _ _ _ _ _ _

NUPTEAS

_ _ _ _ _ _ _

Solution is on page 52.

Connect the Dots #2

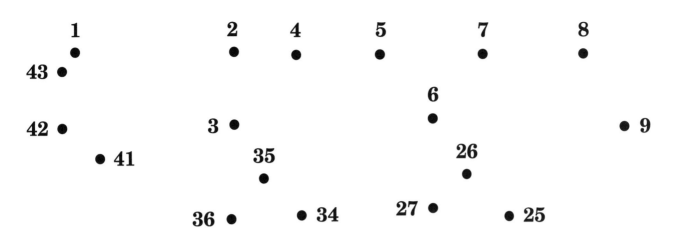

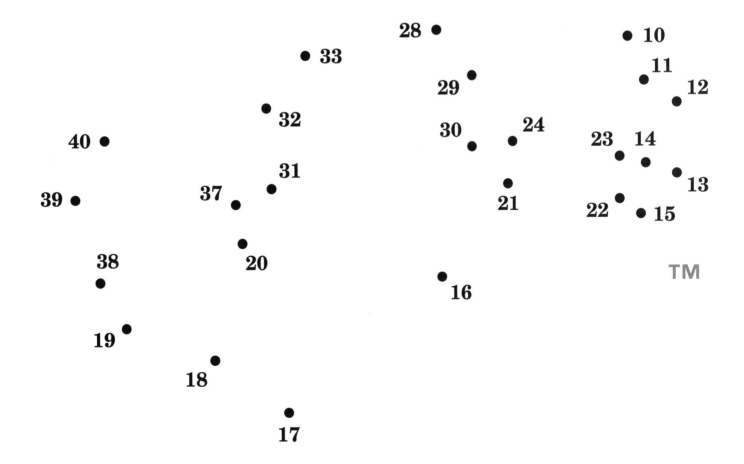

Color the *Twins* logo!

Coloring Page

The *Twins* Mascot

Word Search #1

```
T E R R I T O R Y X Z
N T C M E H M K W Y B
A M I N N E S O T A M
V D T C B E A R T Y T
Y T I W W V O F D E S
B O E T Y U E L G A K
L N S Q W W E R L Y M
U H R K N I A T K B O
E A V T F T N N U E S
R A Q G X S A S U B T
F N I Q R H O R A O E
```

Try to find all the words contained in the list below:

CITIES	MINNESOTA	T.C. BEAR
FIELD	NAVY BLUE	TERRITORY
HANKY	TARGET	TWINS

Solution is on page 53.

Coloring Page

Batter up!

Crossword Puzzle #1 – Baseball Facts

Use your knowledge about baseball facts to solve the crossword puzzle.

Across

1. The pitcher stands on the pitcher's _____ when he throws the baseball.

5. After the batter hits the ball, he runs toward _____ base.

6. The player who throws the ball toward home plate for the batter to hit is called the _____.

9. To score a run, the player must touch _____ plate.

Down

2. The _____ calls the balls and strikes.

3. Each baseball player wears a baseball _____ on his head.

4. Three strikes and you're _____!

7. The player who crouches behind home plate is called the _____.

8. A baseball player wears a _____ on his hand to catch the ball.

Crossword Puzzle #1 – Baseball Facts

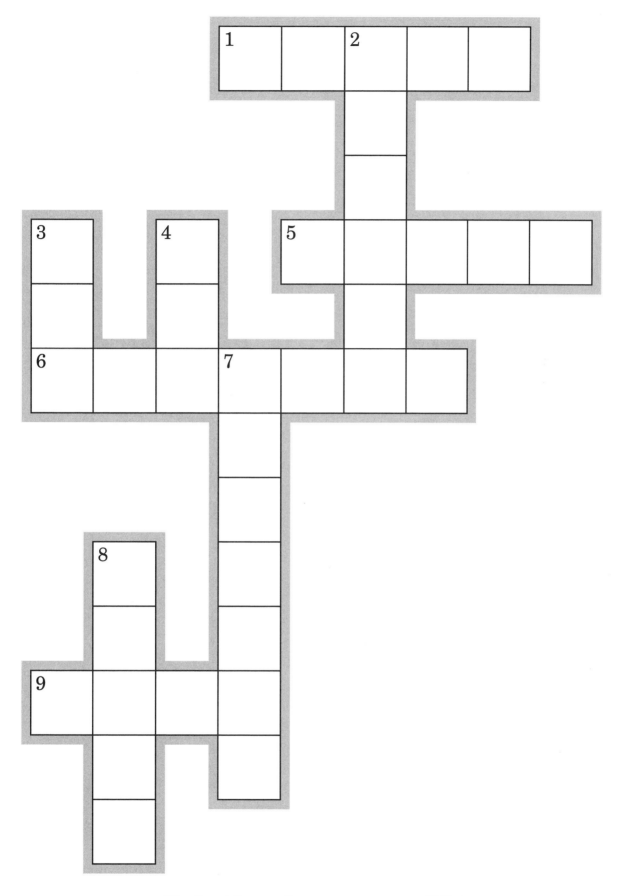

Solution is on page 53.

Connect the Dots #3

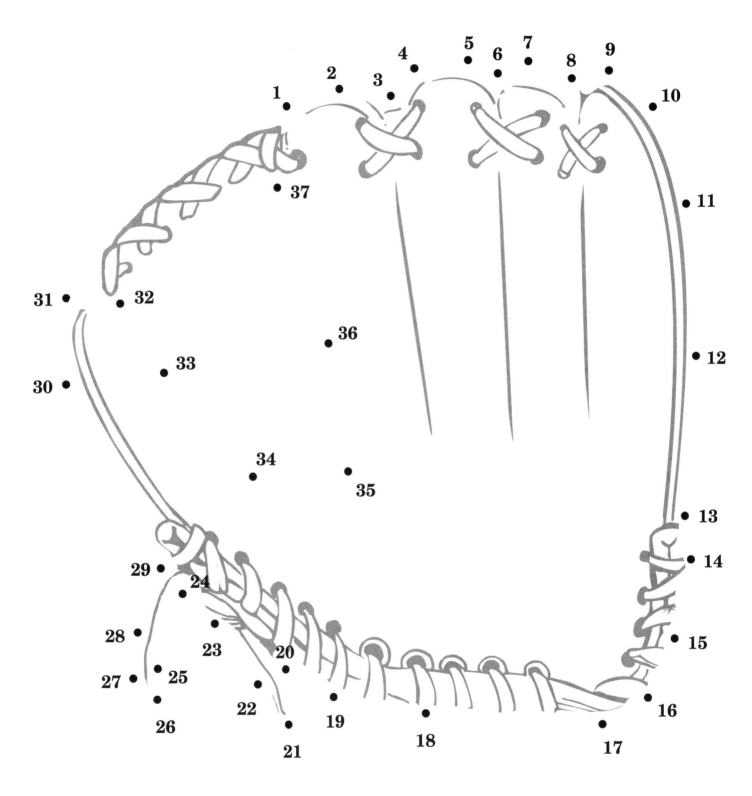

My Day at the Ballpark

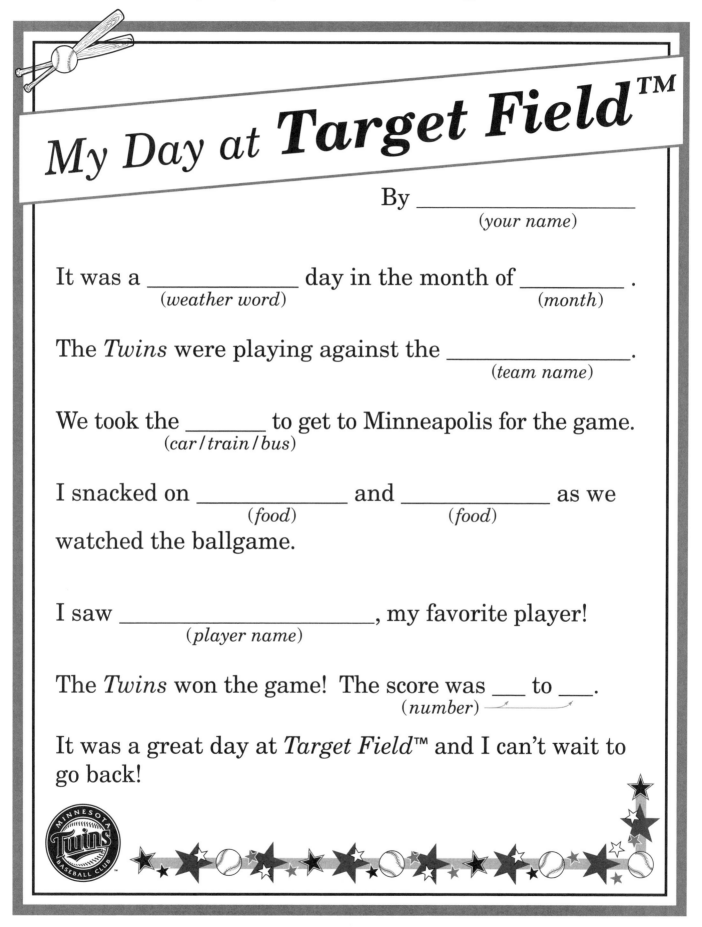

My Day at **Target Field**™

By _____
(your name)

It was a _____ day in the month of _____ .
(weather word)   *(month)*

The *Twins* were playing against the _____.
(team name)

We took the _____ to get to Minneapolis for the game.
(car / train / bus)

I snacked on _____ and _____ as we
(food)   *(food)*
watched the ballgame.

I saw _____, my favorite player!
(player name)

The *Twins* won the game! The score was ___ to ___.
(number)

It was a great day at *Target Field*™ and I can't wait to
go back!

Coloring Page

Yummy Stadium Snacks

Coloring Page

A Home Run Swing!

Baseball Words Scramble

Unscramble the letters to reveal the names of these baseball words.

TBA

_ _ _

APC

_ _ _

PMRIEU

_ _ _ _ _ _

SYERJE

_ _ _ _ _ _

VOEGL

_ _ _ _ _

EBAS

_ _ _ _

Solution is on page 54.

Follow the Ball #2

Circle the batter whose ball was caught by the outfielder.

Solution is on page 54.

Secret Message #2

Use the key to unscramble this message.

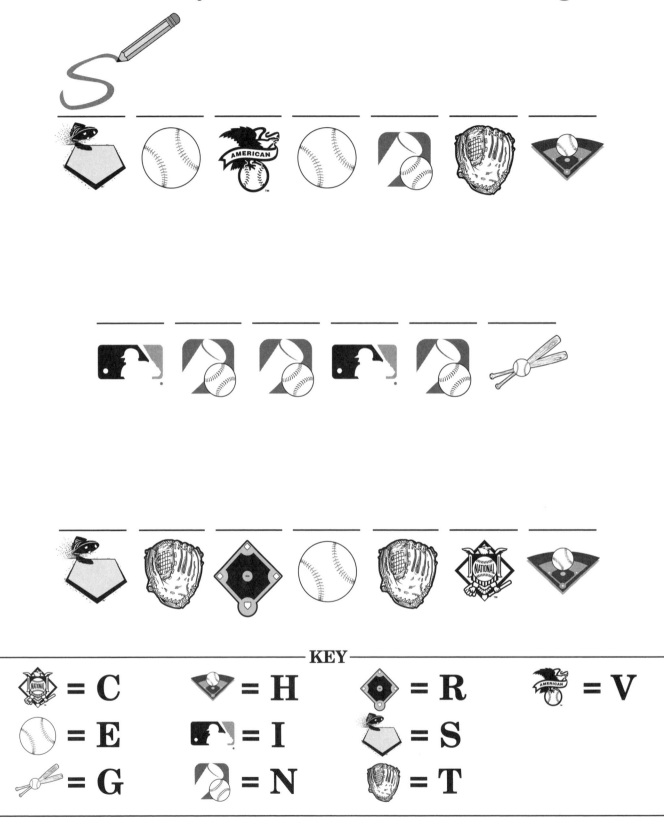

Solution: SEVENTH INNING STRETCH

KEY

National = C
baseball = E
bats = G
field = H
MLB = I
N-ball = N
diamond = R
home plate = S
glove = T
American = V

Solution is on page 55.

Word Search #2

```
T T P L A Y O F F S D
E W U T H I D E N N N
O S E P F G C O S A M
B E O N W Y I R C S W
F R L U A P A I M G G
T I M D M T R U Q B R
H E V A S E I Y W F X
D S H L M D B O L X T
Y C L A A R Z U N W U
C A F T E Y X Q Q A X
V S S D E R O Z O U L
```

Try to find all the words contained in the list below:

ALL STARS	DERBY	SERIES
AMERICAN	NATIONAL	STADIUMS
CHAMPIONS	PLAYOFFS	TROPHY

Solution is on page 55.

Hidden Picture #1

Secret Message #3

Use the key to unscramble this message.

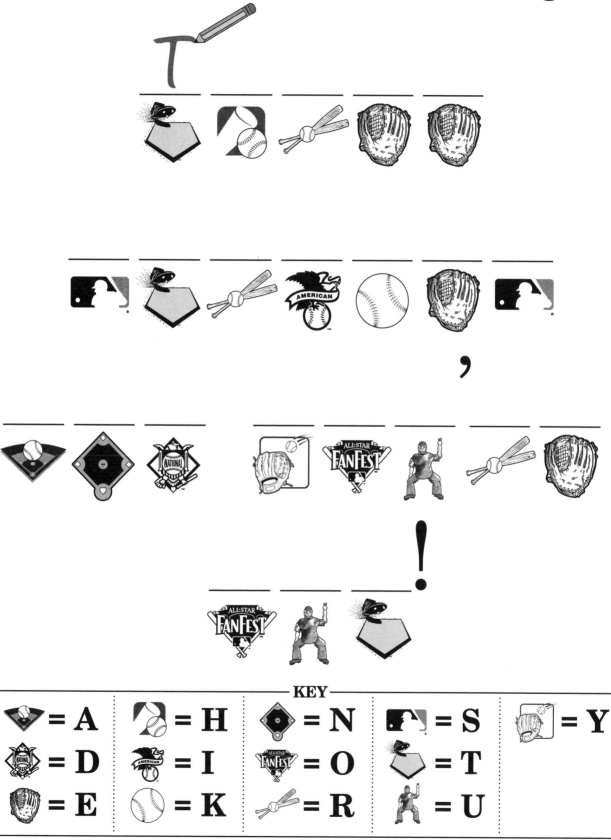

THREE

STRIKES,

AND YOU'RE

OUT!

KEY

= A	= H	= N	= S	= Y
= D	= I	= O	= T	
= E	= K	= R	= U	

Solution is on page 56.

Coloring Page

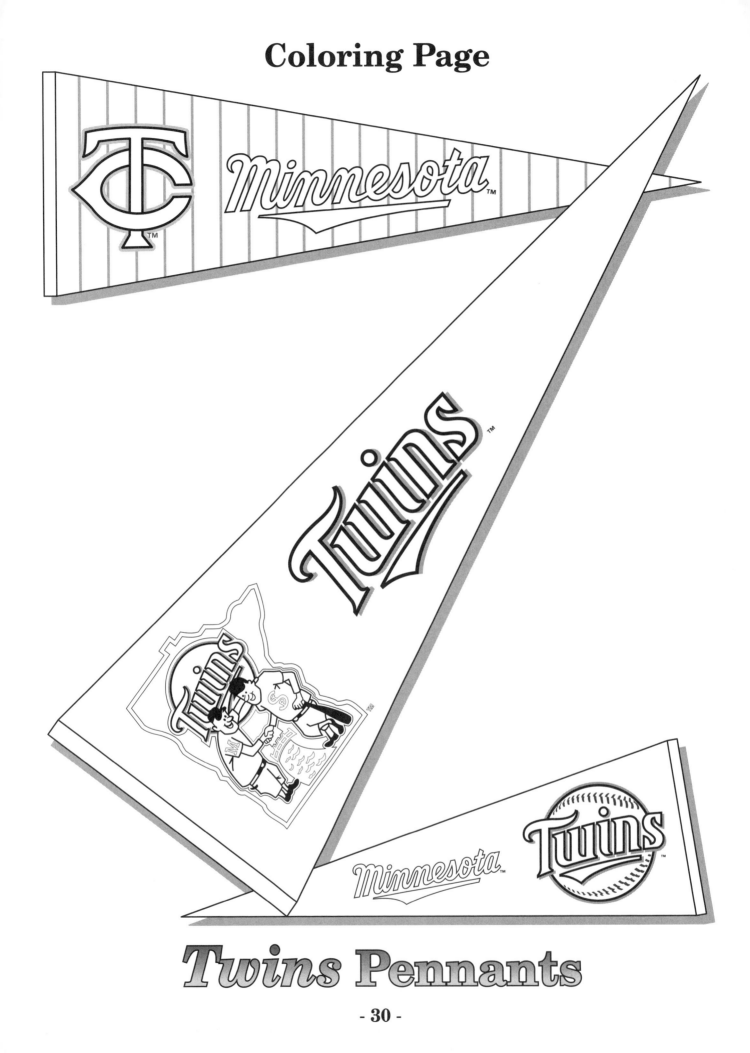

Twins Pennants

What's Inside *"Minnesota Twins?"*

Make 20 new words using the letters contained in the words *"Minnesota Twins."*

MINNESOTA TWINS

Example: NEON

Example: SEAT

1. _____
2. _____
3. _____
4. _____
5. _____
6. _____
7. _____
8. _____
9. _____
10. _____

11. _____
12. _____
13. _____
14. _____
15. _____
16. _____
17. _____
18. _____
19. _____
20. _____

Solution is on page 56.

My Page About Me

My name is _____.

My age is ____.

My favorite team is _____.

My favorite player is _____.

My favorite position to play is _____.

I bat (righty / lefty).

I throw (righty / lefty).

My favorite number is ____.

Coloring Page

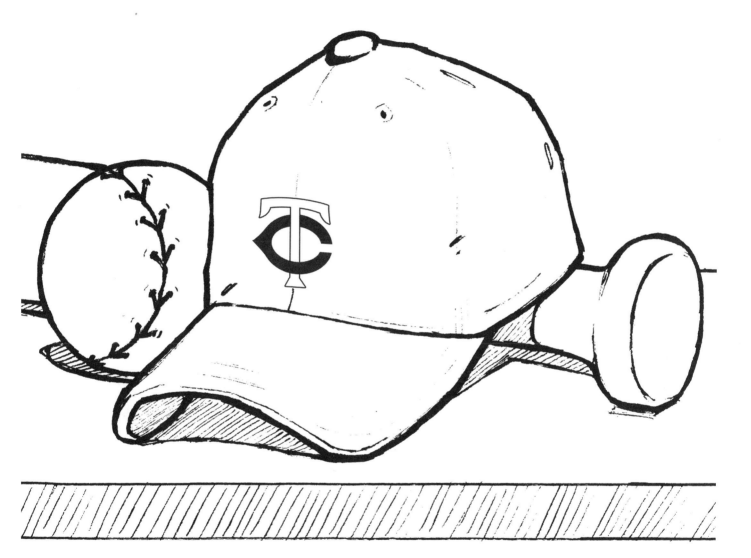

What's the Score?

Add the runs to see who wins.

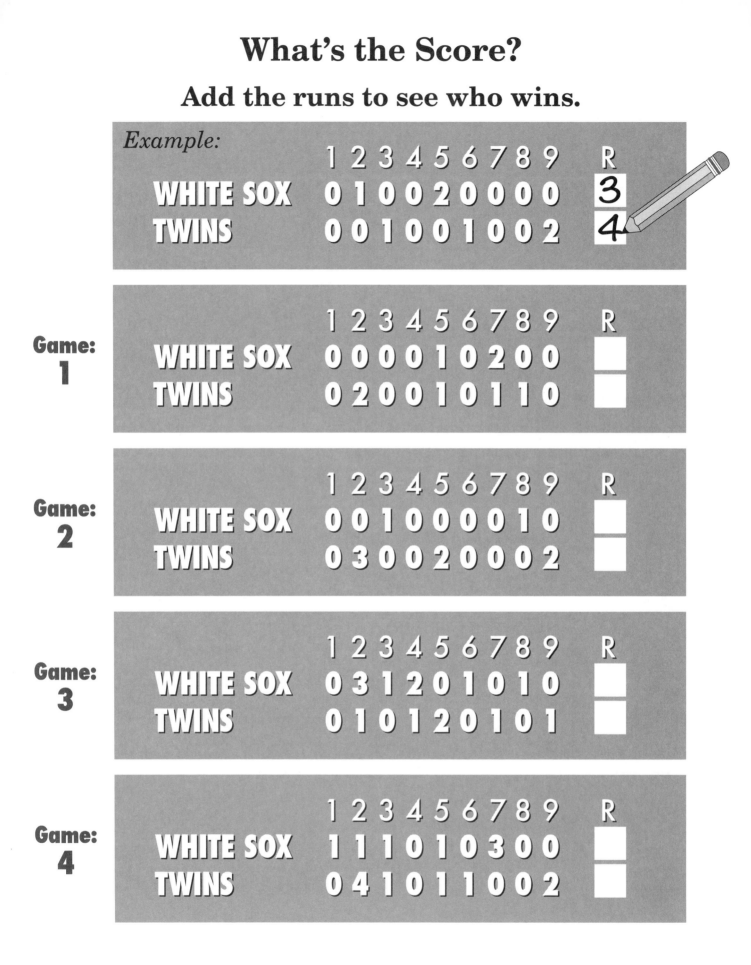

Example:

	1	2	3	4	5	6	7	8	9	R
WHITE SOX	0	1	0	0	2	0	0	0	0	**3**
TWINS	0	0	1	0	0	1	0	0	2	**4**

Game: 1

	1	2	3	4	5	6	7	8	9	R
WHITE SOX	0	0	0	0	1	0	2	0	0	
TWINS	0	2	0	0	1	0	1	1	0	

Game: 2

	1	2	3	4	5	6	7	8	9	R
WHITE SOX	0	0	1	0	0	0	0	1	0	
TWINS	0	3	0	0	2	0	0	0	2	

Game: 3

	1	2	3	4	5	6	7	8	9	R
WHITE SOX	0	3	1	2	0	1	0	1	0	
TWINS	0	1	0	1	2	0	1	0	1	

Game: 4

	1	2	3	4	5	6	7	8	9	R
WHITE SOX	1	1	1	0	1	0	3	0	0	
TWINS	0	4	1	0	1	1	0	0	2	

Solution is on page 57.

Maze #2

Solution is on page 57.

Draw the *MLB* Logo

Use the grid to help you draw the *MLB* logo!

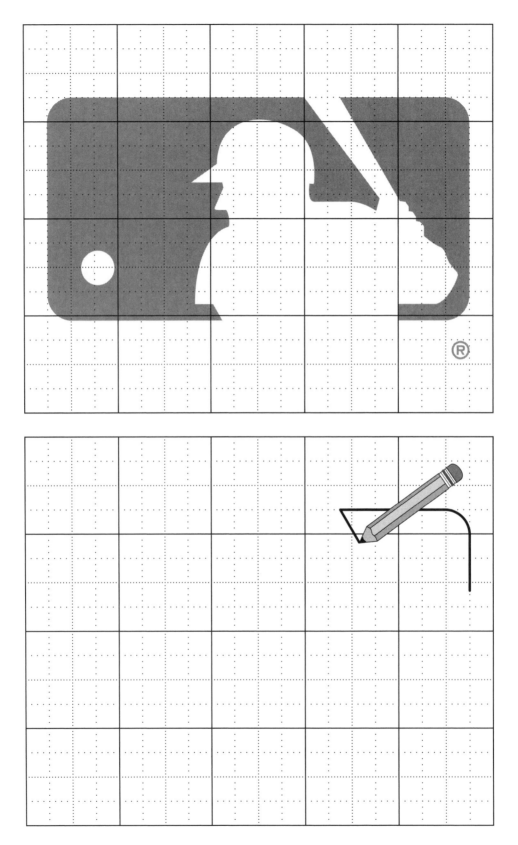

Word Search #3

```
K  G  R  I  F  F  I  T  H  V  K
A  Q  S  F  F  V  T  V  K  S  S
F  K  I  L  L  E  B  R  E  W  Y
Z  I  L  V  K  L  H  T  E  D  A
N  J  U  C  U  Y  N  R  N  B  A
C  E  U  A  H  O  A  C  B  V  N
B  P  J  R  B  C  K  D  I  E  A
O  I  M  N  O  J  H  L  J  N  K
M  A  U  E  R  H  O  M  Z  F  I
V  V  E  A  Y  S  D  I  Q  S  S
Y  M  O  L  I  T  O  R  G  F  K
```

Try to find all the words contained in the list below:

CAREW	HRBEK	MOLITOR
CARNEAL	KILLEBREW	PUCKETT
GRIFFITH	MAUER	OLIVA

Solution is on page 58.

Coloring Page

One Lucky Twins Fan!

Secret Message #4

Use the key to unscramble this message.

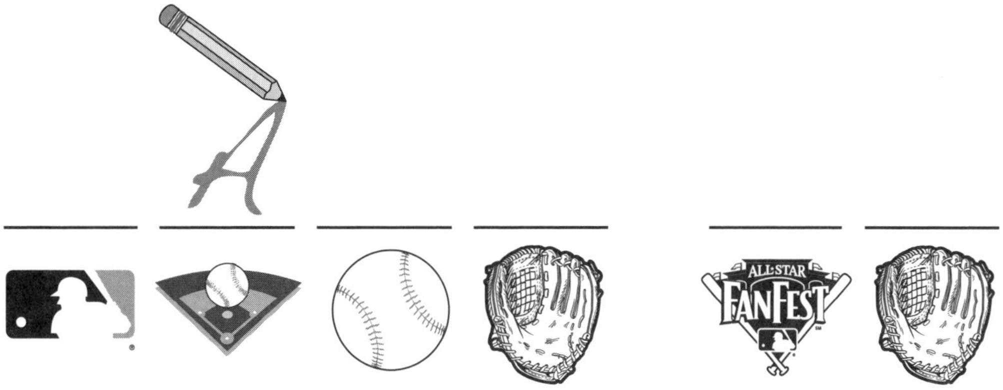

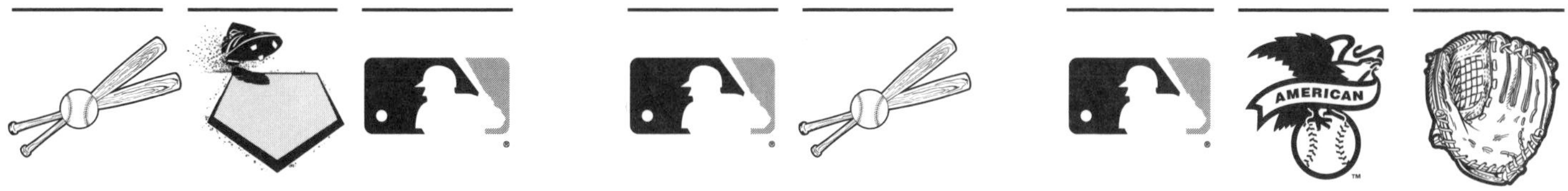

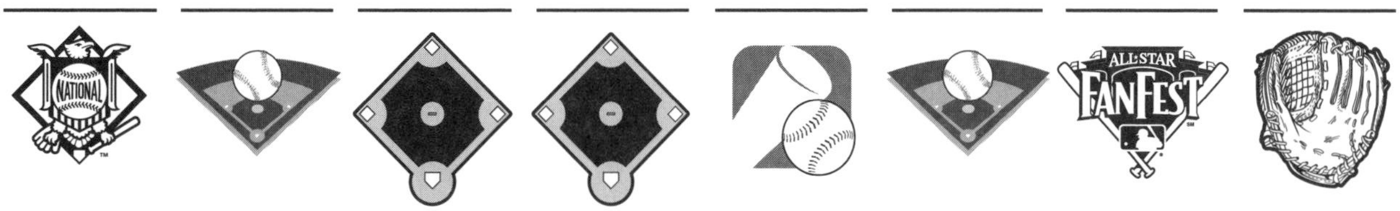

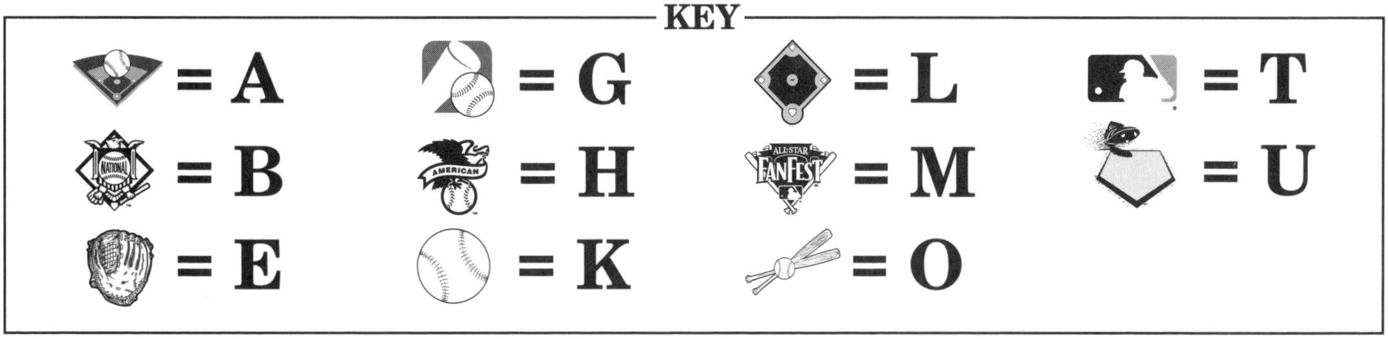

Solution is on page 58.

Find the Differences #3

Find four differences between the two images.

Solution is on page 59.

Baseball Positions Scramble

Unscramble the letters to reveal the names of these baseball positions.

ITCHREP
PITCHER

RIFTS
_ _ _ _ _ _

SABMANE
_ _ _ _ _ _ _

CAHTERC
_ _ _ _ _ _ _

ERTTAB
_ _ _ _ _ _

TUOLIEFDRE
_ _ _ _ _ _ _ _ _ _

Solution is on page 59.

What's Inside *"Major League Baseball?"*

Make 20 new words using the letters contained in the words *"Major League Baseball."*

MAJOR LEAGUE BASEBALL

Example: AREA

Example: BEAR

1 _____

2 _____

3 _____

4 _____

5 _____

6 _____

7 _____

8 _____

9 _____

10 _____

11 _____

12 _____

13 _____

14 _____

15 _____

16 _____

17 _____

18 _____

19 _____

20 _____

Solution is on page 60.

Maze #3

Follow the maze to the correct exit to find out if the batter is out or safe.

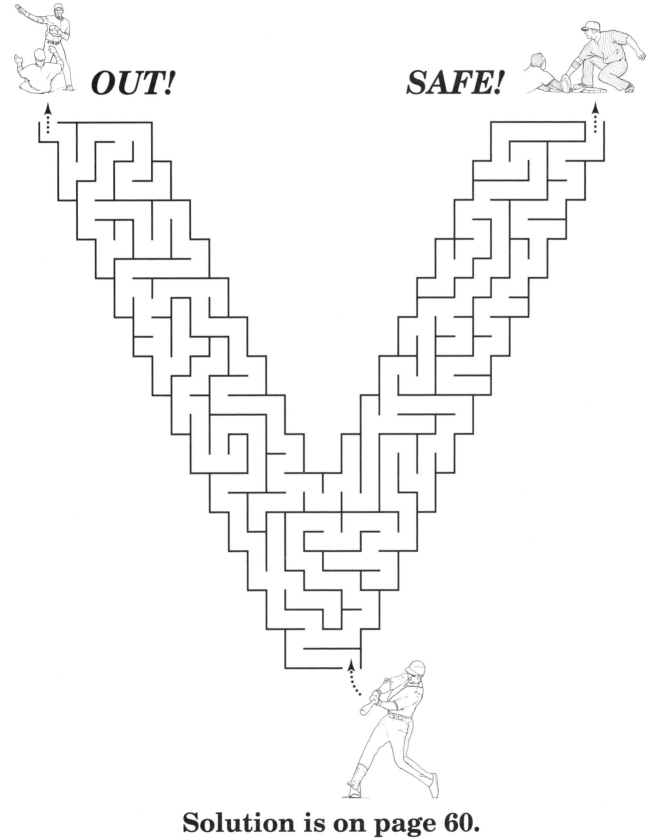

OUT!

SAFE!

Solution is on page 60.

Crossword Puzzle #2 – *Twins* Facts

Use your knowledge about the *Twins* Facts to solve the crossword puzzle.

Across

3. Burt Blyleven, Frank Viola, and Jim Perry were all famous *Twins* _____.

4. *T.C. Bear* is the name of the *Twins* _____.

6. The home of the *Twins* is _____ *Field*.

7. The *Twins* are named after the twin cities of St. Paul and _____.

Down

1. Hall of Famer Kirby _____ wore number 34 for the *Twins*.

2. In 1991, the *Twins* defeated the _____ in extra innings in the seventh game to win the *World Series*.

5. The *Twins* play in the _____ *League*.

Crossword Puzzle #2 – *Twins* Facts

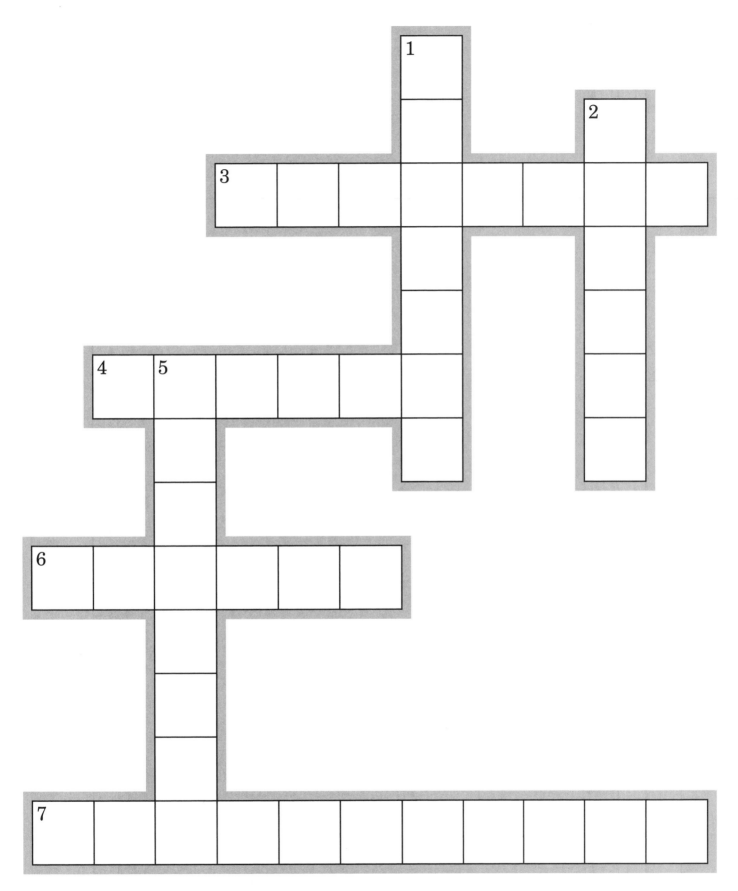

Solution is on page 61.

Hidden Picture #2

KEY

A = Dark Blue   B = Light Blue   C = Light Grey   D = Dark Grey (or black)   E = Tan

Word Search #4

C T J I Q U E K R R W
P A I U D L Z K T L V
E M T G P U H C U P B
N Z S C M B G O A T A
U P Y T H L F O K P S
C C D U R E Y B U I E
F V W U R I R S I T B
O W K I O V K E R C A
Q X P G L O V E Q H L
E M Z D R G Z X T E L
U Z S O G S M T N R Q

Try to find all the words contained in the list below:

BASEBALL	DUGOUT	PITCHER
CAP	FOUL	STRIKE
CATCHER	GLOVE	UMPIRE

Solution is on page 61.

Find the Difference #4

Circle the image that is different.

Solution is on page 62.

Solutions to Puzzles
Solution to Retired Heroes Game, page 2

Solution to Follow the Ball #1, page 3

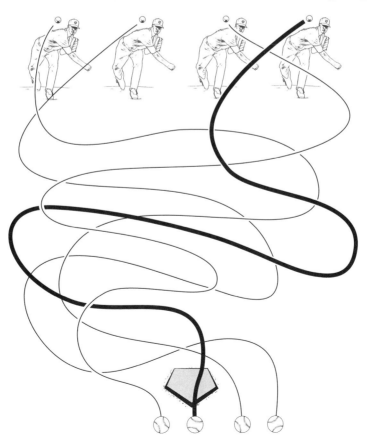

Solution to Find the Differences #1, page 5

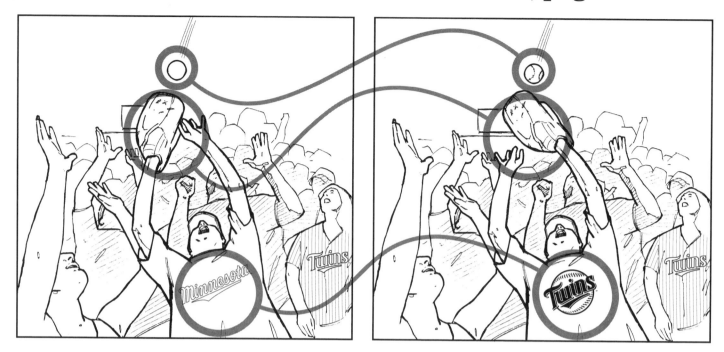

Solution to Maze #1, page 6

Solution to Find the Difference #2, page 7

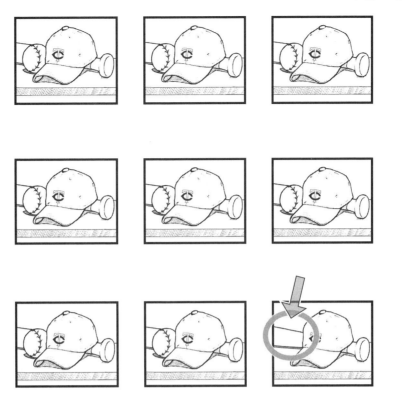

Solution to Secret Message #1, page 9

Solution to Label the Parts of a Baseball Field, page 10

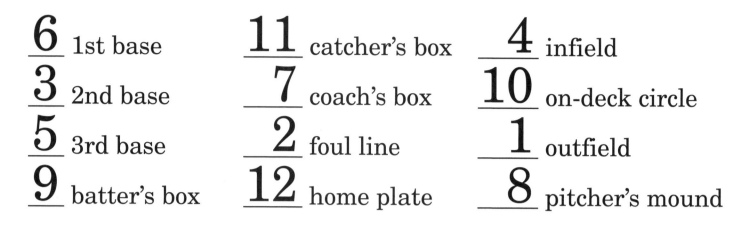

__6__ 1st base   __11__ catcher's box   __4__ infield

__3__ 2nd base   __7__ coach's box   __10__ on-deck circle

__5__ 3rd base   __2__ foul line   __1__ outfield

__9__ batter's box   __12__ home plate   __8__ pitcher's mound

Solution to Stadium Snacks Scramble, page 12

SODA

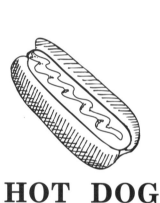

HOT DOG

POPCORN

ICE CREAM

PRETZEL

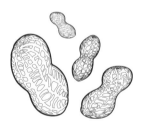

PEANUTS

Solution to Word Search #1, page 16

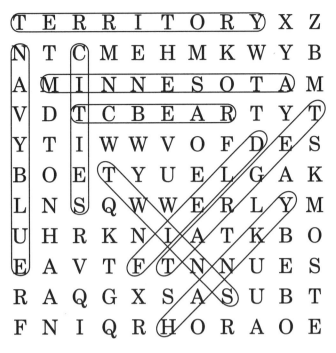

Try to find all the words contained in the list below:

CITIES	MINNESOTA	T.C. BEAR
FIELD	NAVY BLUE	TERRITORY
HANKY	TARGET	TWINS

Solution to Crossword Puzzle #1 - Baseball Facts, page 19

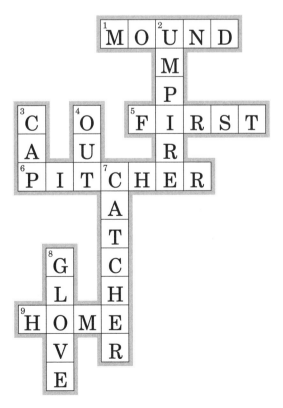

Solution to Baseball Words Scramble, page 24

BAT

CAP

UMPIRE

JERSEY

GLOVE

BASE

Solution to Follow the Ball #2, page 25

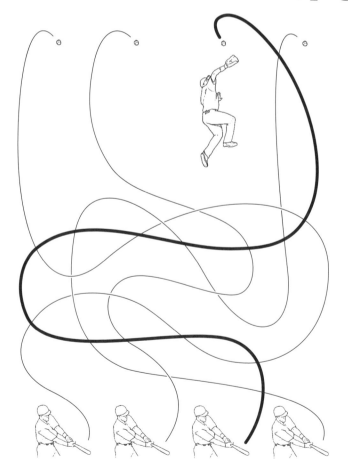

Solution to Secret Message #2, page 26

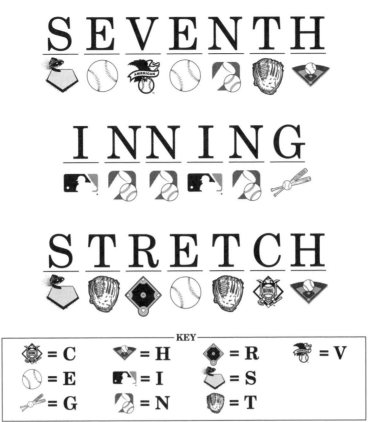

S E V E N T H

I N N I N G

S T R E T C H

KEY

= C		= H		= R		= V	
= E		= I		= S			
= G		= N		= T			

Solution Word Search #2, page 27

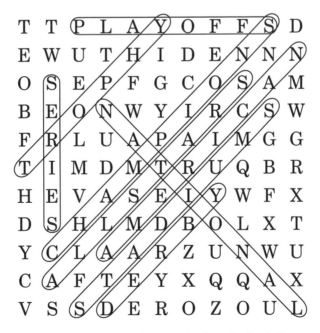

Try to find all the words contained in the list below:

ALL STARS	DERBY	SERIES
AMERICAN	NATIONAL	STADIUMS
CHAMPIONS	PLAYOFFS	TROPHY

Solution to What's Inside *Minnesota Twins*, page 31

Below are just a few examples of words that could be made with these letters.

M I N N E S O T A   T W I N S

asset	meant	moan	note	some	taste	town
atom	meat	moat	nose	state	team	wait
east	meow	most	omit	steam	tent	want
into	mess	mown	saint	stem	test	wean
item	mine	name	same	stone	time	went
main	mini	neat	sane	swam	tint	west
mass	mint	nine	seam	swat	toast	win
mast	mist	noise	sent	swim	tone	wine
mean	mitt	none	site	tame	toss	wise

Solution to What's the Score?, page 34

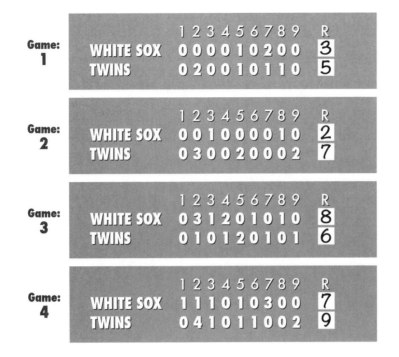

Game: 1

	1	2	3	4	5	6	7	8	9	R
WHITE SOX	0	0	0	0	1	0	2	0	0	3
TWINS	0	2	0	0	1	0	1	1	0	5

Game: 2

	1	2	3	4	5	6	7	8	9	R
WHITE SOX	0	0	1	0	0	0	0	1	0	2
TWINS	0	3	0	0	2	0	0	0	2	7

Game: 3

	1	2	3	4	5	6	7	8	9	R
WHITE SOX	0	3	1	2	0	1	0	1	0	8
TWINS	0	1	0	1	2	0	1	0	1	6

Game: 4

	1	2	3	4	5	6	7	8	9	R
WHITE SOX	1	1	1	0	1	0	3	0	0	7
TWINS	0	4	1	0	1	1	0	0	2	9

Solution to Maze #2, page 35

Solution to Word Search #3, page 37

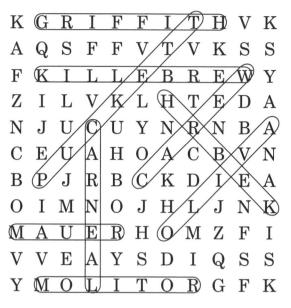

```
K G R I F F I T H V K
A Q S F F V T V K S S
F K I L L E B R E W Y
Z I L V K L H T E D A
N J U C U Y N R N B A
C E U A H O A C B V N
B P J R B C K D I E A
O I M N O J H L J N K
M A U E R H O M Z F I
V V E A Y S D I Q S S
Y M O L I T O R G F K
```

Try to find all the words contained in the list below:

CAREW	HRBEK	MOLITOR
CARNEAL	KILLEBREW	PUCKETT
GRIFFITH	MAUER	OLIVA

Solution to Secret Message #4, page 39

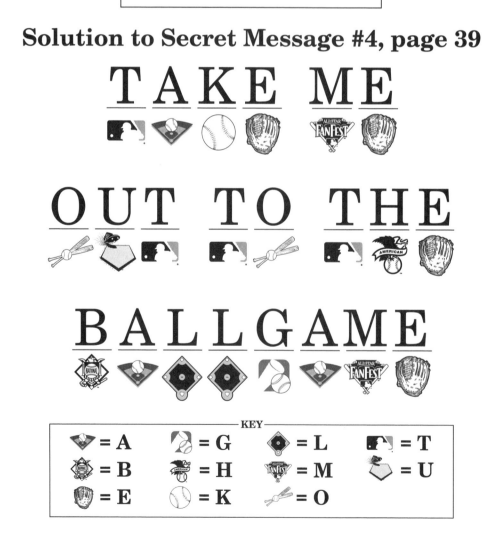

TAKE ME

OUT TO THE

BALLGAME

KEY

= A	= G	= L	= T
= B	= H	= M	= U
= E	= K	= O	

Solution to Find the Differences #3, page 40

Solution to Baseball Positions Scramble, page 41

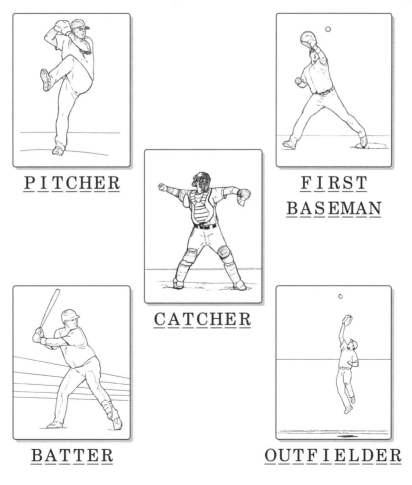

PITCHER

FIRST BASEMAN

CATCHER

BATTER

OUTFIELDER

MAJOR LEAGUE BASEBALL

ajar	beam	bull	gore	meal	reel	seem
alas	bear	ease	lamb	mole	roll	sell
also	bell	else	lame	mule	rule	slab
area	blob	game	lobe	muse	saga	slam
aura	blue	gear	lube	ogre	sage	soar
ball	blur	germ	lure	oral	sale	some
barb	boar	glee	male	rage	seal	sour
bare	bomb	glue	mall	real	seam	urge
base	bulb	goal	mars	ream	sear	user

Solution to Maze #3, page 43

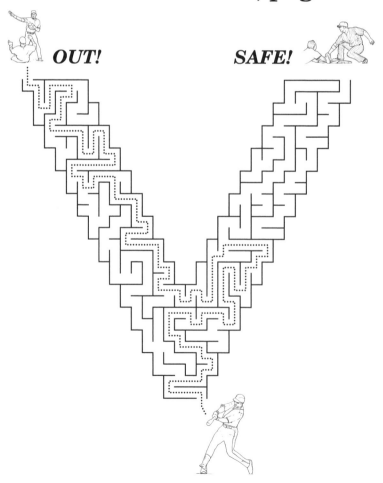

OUT!   SAFE!

Solution to Crossword #2 - *Twins* Facts, page 45

Solution to Word Search #4, page 47

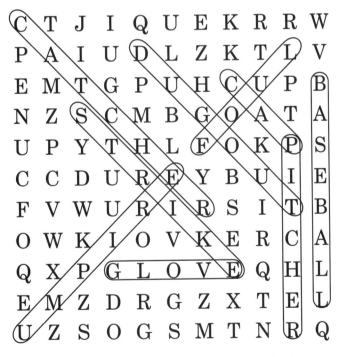

Try to find all the words contained in the list below:

BASEBALL	DUGOUT	PITCHER
CAP	FOUL	STRIKE
CATCHER	GLOVE	UMPIRE

Solution to Find the Difference #4, page 48

 We hope that you enjoyed the
Minnesota Twins
Activity Book!

Please contact us with questions or comments:

Hawk's Nest Publishing LLC
85 B Wall Street
Madison, CT 06443
www.HawksNestPublishing.com
facebook.com/HawksNestPub
Twitter: @HawksNestPub

Books for the Young and Young at Heart...